# PRAISE

"Cheryl Goss empowers all of us standing at life's crossroads to know we're not alone. She shares her story with vulnerability and hard-won wisdom, inviting us to blossom in our own hard stories, not just in spite of our great struggles but because of them."
  - KATHERINE WOLF, author of *Suffer Strong* and *Hope Heals*

"Cheryl Goss writes from the heart, from the Word, and from the many times she faced a crossroad in her life. Her journey has been difficult, and yet what she learned along those rocky roads paved the way for her vital ministry to women. Cheryl's message of grace is clear, and her encouragement to share our own stories is empowering. *Crossroads* is a gift to all of us who need to know that God is good, and that His mercy is more than enough to cover all our sins."
  - LIZ CURTIS HIGGS, best-selling author of *Bad Girls of the Bible*

"Cheryl Goss's *Crossroads* is truly an example of strength being displayed through weakness. Cheryl's writing is rich with truth as well as relatable. She takes the gospel as truth while also making the reader feel as if they are a new friend. You will laugh, you might cry, but you will certainly be encouraged."
  - MORGAN CHEEK, author of *On Milk and Honey*

"If you've ever felt like you have fallen too far for God to love you, *Crossroads* is for you. Cheryl courageously shares her story of addiction, abuse, and setbacks to demonstrate the awesome power of God's saving grace. In her testimony, she openly confesses her past failures and illustrates that obedience can bring blessing, and admitting weakness is strength. She challenges the reader to stop living in fear of their own 'thorns' and to instead ask God to use them to further His kingdom. Cheryl's journey proves that no one is too far gone to be reached by the saving power of Jesus. Her words offer grace and encouragement to anyone who has ever doubted their worth."

- STARLA CANNING, Connecting Ministries Devotional Team Leader


"Cheryl has made herself vulnerable by sharing her story in this book. She has shown incredible strength by doing so. She has also demonstrated her strong faith in our gracious, merciful God, and has revealed how He has used her thorns for His glory."

- JEAN BYRD, mentor and sister in Christ


"Cheryl Goss has been a friend to me for over ten years. During this time, I have seen her grow in her faith and her calling to use her story to help others. She has been an inspiration to me and so many others. In telling her story, she is unashamedly giving God all the glory in hopes that it will help others. Reading this book encouraged me, made me cry, and I learned more about God's grace, mercy, and forgiveness. She writes from her heart, and I am proud to call her friend."

- MARY MARTHA REYNOLDS, mentor and sister in Christ

# CROSSROADS

# CROSSROADS
A Story of Addictions, Abuse, and Redemption

CHERYL GOSS

Copyright © 2020 by **Cheryl Goss**

All rights reserved. No part of this publication may be reproduced, distributed or transmitted in any form or by any means, without prior written permission.

**Cheryl Goss/Connecting Ministries**
connectingministries.org
info@connectingministries.org

Unless otherwise indicated, all Scripture quotations are taken from the Holy Bible, New Living Translation, copyright © 1996, 2004, 2015 by Tyndale House Foundation. Used by permission of Tyndale House Publishers, a Division of Tyndale House Ministries, Carol Stream, Illinois 60188. All rights reserved.

Some content taken from The Life Application Study Bible Notes and Bible Helps by Tyndale House Publishers. Copyright © 1986, 1988, 1989, 1990, 1991, 1993, 1996, 2004. Used by permission of Tyndale House Publishers, a Division of Tyndale House Ministries. All rights reserved.

Shirer, Priscilla. *Fervent: A Woman's Battle Plan for Serious, Specific, and Strategic Prayer.* Nashville: B&H Publishing Group, 2015. Used by permission.

Cover Design | Ashlee Nocita
Editor | Danelle Young
Proofreader | Pamela Cosel, ATX Editing
Book Layout © 2017 BookDesignTemplates.com

**Crossroads/ Cheryl Goss**. -- 1st ed.
Paperback ISBN 978-1-7348924-2-0
eBook ISBN 978-1-7348924-1-3

# DEDICATION

To my husband, Ryan, for not giving up on me when I was on the wrong road, for showing me to Christ, and for encouraging me to walk in faith even when I doubted my destination.

To my son, Timothy, for being one of the strongest men I know. You have overcome, and you will continue to do so when your eyes are set on Him.

To my daughters, Peyton, Layla, and Mia, thank you for loving Christ the way you do, and for showing me and others how beautiful that love is.

You are all a representation of Christ's love. Thank you for patiently allowing me to pursue my calling. Doing ministry with you is a blessing, and one that I will cherish forever. Continue to seek your heavenly Father and listen for His voice.

*"This is what the Lord says:*
*'Stop at the crossroads and look around.*
*Ask for the old, godly way, and walk in it.*
*Travel its path, and you will find rest for your souls.'*
*But you reply, 'No, that's not the road we want!'"*

JEREMIAH 6:16

# CONTENTS

ACKNOWLEDGMENTS ................................................................xiii
INTRODUCTION ........................................................................ xv
THORNS.......................................................................................1
IN THE BEGINNING ...................................................................9
WHICH WAY?..........................................................................17
NOT AGAIN .............................................................................23
I'VE BEEN WAITING ON YOU ...............................................29
BUT, GOD? ..............................................................................35
CROSSROADS .........................................................................41
   REFLECTION ONE + CROSSROAD EXAMINATION .....43
SHARING YOUR STORY ........................................................45
   REFLECTION TWO + ENCOURAGE A FRIEND.............48
WALKING IN FAITH ..............................................................51
   REFLECTION THREE + YOUR NEXT STEP...................55
FERVENT PRAYER..................................................................57
   REFLECTION FOUR + SUITING UP .................................65
IN THE END .............................................................................67
YOUR THORNS, YOUR STORY .............................................75
   REFLECTION FIVE + YOUR STORY................................77
ABOUT THE AUTHOR ............................................................83

# ACKNOWLEDGMENTS

I want to thank everyone who prayed with me and for me through the creation of *Crossroads*. I can't begin to list names, but you know who you are.

I also want to thank:

Danelle Young, for editing and formatting this book. You, by far, have had the hardest job. You've been an answer to prayer and encouraging through it all.

Starla Canning, for checking biblical accuracy, and for giving me strength when I didn't want to continue.

Connecting Ministries Board of Directors, for walking and praying with me through this ministry journey. Each one of you bless and encourage me.

Julie Dunn, for being one of my biggest cheerleaders! I love you.

Jean Byrd and Mary Martha Reynolds, for praying, guiding, and encouraging me in ministry.

Ashlee Nocita, you are a woman of many gifts and talents. Thank you for being a great friend, mentor and assistant but most importantly, thank you for loving Jesus the way you do and allowing Him to use you.

My gals at FOS, for allowing me to come and share life with you. Our time together inspired me to write this book. Each one of you played a pivotal part. You are loved greatly, and you have blessed my life abundantly.

# INTRODUCTION

When I stepped into ministry ten years ago, God revealed to me that people within my church and community were hurting. I learned that some of my brothers and sisters in Christ were battling addictions, abuse, depression, marriage issues, and the list could go on. My empathy for these individuals, especially women, grew as God opened doors for me to share my story with different groups. When I started to walk forward in faith, my life's purpose came into focus. A women's ministry position quickly turned into a journey of understanding and claiming my own God story.

Followers of Jesus come from various backgrounds. Some of us were raised in broken or single-parent homes. Others come from good homes but did not grow up in the church. Some went to church but did not have a personal relationship with Jesus until later in life. And a number of you were blessed to be brought up in Christian homes and have walked with Jesus since childhood. But trials don't discriminate, and the enemy is intentional about using our weaknesses against us. We must all be aware of the spiritual battle surrounding each of us.

While writing this book and thinking back on my childhood and young adult years, a range of thoughts and emotions surfaced, some of which the enemy used to slow me down. I have prayed fervently for this book, for my family, for myself, and for everyone who picks up *Crossroads* to read. I don't want to make anyone feel bad or to point fingers regarding my childhood. I know how that feels. I simply want to share my story in hopes that it will aid those who are searching for meaning in life or who may have lost faith in the One True God. This book is also for readers who are pushing through difficult circumstances. Life is hard, and it can be messy. Jesus didn't say our faith walk would be easy, but He promised to be with us every step of the way. I share my story with you to demonstrate that through Christ, we can overcome our circumstances!

Helping women see their struggles and sins as opportunities to rely on Christ is my passion. I fear that many in the church are slowly losing hope and faith in Christ. My intention here is to encourage you, the reader, to see your past and present circumstances in a new and purposeful light. My heart goes out to all of you. My prayer is that you read this and understand that you, as a child of God, have a beautiful story. Claim it and use it for His glory! And may seeds of our Savior's love and faithfulness grow within you and sustain you through the crossroads in your life.

CHAPTER ONE

# THORNS

Thank you for picking up this book! I sat down numerous times over the years, trying to put pen to paper. I attempted to type but would only be able to punch out a sentence or two. I'm not sure why it's been so hard. I eventually started questioning myself: *Is it that I'm afraid of my own story? Afraid of reliving some of those dark days? Fearful of the enemy trying to capitalize on my insecurities? Am I concerned readers will judge me because of my past (my journey to Christ)?* I concluded that by not writing, I was allowing the enemy to use my insecurities to keep me frozen in fear. These words, this book, well, it's my story—the story that God has given me. And I feel He is leading me to share it with you.

While writing recently, I've prayed that someone will be encouraged by what I'm about to share. Perhaps someone who is walking through a trial and who needs to hear that God is good. Throughout life, we all come to crossroads, and some of those roads lead us through thorny territory. In the book of 2 Corinthians, Paul describes the painful prick of a "thorn" in his flesh.

## 2 · THORNS

> *Paul's Vision and His Thorn in the Flesh*
>
> *This boasting will do no good, but I must go on. I will reluctantly tell about visions and revelations from the Lord. I was caught up to the third heaven fourteen years ago. Whether I was in my body or out of my body, I don't know—only God knows. Yes, only God knows whether I was in my body or outside my body. But I do know that I was caught up to paradise and heard things so astounding that they cannot be expressed in words, things no human is allowed to tell. That experience is worth boasting about, but I'm not going to do it. I will boast only about my weaknesses. If I wanted to boast, I would be no fool in doing so, because I would be telling the truth. But I won't do it, because I don't want anyone to give me credit beyond what they can see in my life or hear in my message, even though I have received such wonderful revelations from God. So, to keep me from becoming proud, I was given a thorn in my flesh, a messenger from Satan to torment me and keep me from becoming proud. Three different times I begged the Lord to take it away. Each time he said, "My grace is all you need. My power works best in weakness." So now I am glad to boast about my weaknesses, so that the power of Christ can work through me. That's why I take pleasure in my weaknesses, and in the insults, hardships, persecutions, and troubles that I suffer for Christ. For when I am weak, then I am strong. (2 Corinthians 12:1-10)*

First, we need to understand why this letter was written. Paul penned this letter around 56AD during his third missionary journey.[1] It reveals the heart and spirit of one of the greatest ministers of all time. Which is sometimes hard for me to believe. Wasn't Paul previously known as Saul, the same man who hated and persecuted followers of Jesus? And now we see him writing these beautiful letters. It's amazing how God used a man with a past like Saul's to write so much of His Word (the Bible) to us!

In this letter Paul introduced himself to the Corinthians as "an apostle of Christ Jesus." He wants to make sure the Corinthians understand who he is and why he is doing this. One thing that stands out in this letter is that Paul gets personal. He describes himself more in this letter than any other.[2] Let's re-read and dive deeper. "This boasting will do no good, but I must go on. I will reluctantly tell about visions and revelations from the Lord. I was caught up to the third heaven fourteen years ago. Whether I was in my body or out of my body, I don't know—only God knows. Yes, only God knows whether I was in my body or outside my body. But I do know that I was caught up to paradise and heard things so astounding that they cannot be expressed in words, things no human is allowed to tell" (2 Corinthians 12:1-4).

We wonder what Paul is trying to describe here. Is "the third heaven" referring to where God himself lives? Nowhere in the Bible does it explain what he is talking about exactly; however, one commentary I read said that this vision could have occurred during a near-death experience described in Acts 14.[3] Paul and Barnabas were preaching in Iconium, performing miracles, and crediting Christ. Crowds of people believed, however, some didn't like what Paul was saying and doing, so they plotted to stone him.

"Then some Jews arrived from Antioch and Iconium and won the crowds to their side. They stoned Paul and dragged him out of town, thinking he was dead. But as the believers gathered around him, he got up and went back into town. The next day he left with Barnabas for Derbe" (Acts 14:19-20).

The most incredible part of this story is the fact that Paul survived being stoned, got up, and went back into town to preach again. No one could stop him from proclaiming the truth. I love it!

"That experience is worth boasting about, but I'm not going to do it. I will boast only about my weaknesses. If I wanted to boast, I would be no fool in doing so, because I would be telling the truth. But I won't do it, because I don't want anyone to give me credit beyond what they can see in my life or hear in my message, even though I have received such wonderful revelations from God. So to keep me from becoming proud, I was given a thorn in my flesh, a messenger from Satan to torment me and keep me from becoming proud" (2 Corinthians 12:5-7).

Scripture does not describe Paul's thorn; some think it was an eye disease or epilepsy. We do know that it hindered his ministry to the point that some days, Paul was not able to work. But Paul was given that thorn so he would not become proud or arrogant. It was put there so Paul would see his weaknesses and therefore, fully rely on God. Brilliant! Not exactly how I have looked at my thorns in the past.

I have viewed my thorns and wrong paths as weaknesses in my life. And most of the time we see these weaknesses just as they are, areas of life where we do not have strength. I'm pretty sure that a thorn is what kept me from writing these words to you. I truly believe that it's how we view our thorn that will determine how He will use it. You see, Paul was given this thorn in the flesh so He would become reliant on Christ, and we must do the same.

But here's the tricky part: we are sinful people who live in a sinful world. We can easily allow the enemy to use those thorns instead of God. In the past, when facing a crossroad, I often made poor decisions. Consequently, I have been wounded by deep, painful thorns. Looking back, I know God was present at those places, but since I didn't have a relationship with Him, I didn't stop to consult with Him. My childhood and young adult years were confusing and painful. I cried my way through most days. Now that my tears have been wiped away by Jesus, I can fully see Him and His good works and the purpose He has for my life.

"This is what the Lord says: 'Stop at the crossroads and look around. Ask for the old, godly way, and walk in it. Travel its path, and you will find rest for your souls.' But you reply, 'No, that's not the road we want!'" (Jeremiah 6:16).

There are skeletons in my closet that the enemy used to keep me numb, to keep me still, and to keep me from sharing my story. Some of us may struggle through addictions, fears, suicidal thoughts, abuse, or self-worth issues, but what if we choose to look up and set our eyes on the sunrise beyond our thorny surrounding? What if we allow God to take our hand and show us His power? He is waiting to walk with us on to brighter and more purposeful days.

I haven't always been in ministry. I haven't always led a God-fearing life. There were years I carelessly indulged in drugs and alcohol. I've experienced years of abuse and feelings of not being worthy. There are situations and decisions I am not proud of, but God used the resulting thorns to bless me with newfound strength in Him. He's helped me find my voice in order to share just how gracious and loving He's been to me.

No one likes to be uncomfortable or walk through pain. I was okay being numb. There was no reason to address that thorn, right? Wrong! We need to identify our thorns, and this can sometimes be a bit uncomfortable. It can make us realize how dependent we have become on worldly ways instead of God's way. I personally just wanted to ignore my thorn. I didn't want to address it because I knew it could be painful (the reason it has taken me two years to share my story on paper). My thorn has caused me to stand still for too long. The enemy had me right where he wanted me: numb and paralyzed to what God was asking me to do.

"Three different times I begged the Lord to take it away. Each time he said, 'My grace is all you need. My power works best in weakness.' So now I am glad to boast about my weaknesses, so that the power of Christ can work through me. That's why I take pleasure in my weaknesses, and in the insults, hardships, persecutions, and troubles that I suffer for Christ. For when I am weak, then I am strong" (2 Corinthians 12: 8-10).

In my past I have prayed for Him to take away my weaknesses. I have prayed for him to take away my fear, my anxiety, and the pain from my story. I have tried to hide those insecurities, hide parts of my past and hide my thorns. But instead, he's given me a new perspective. I now praise Him for those thorns. I see that He's working through me, giving me the strength to use those thorns to grow the Kingdom of God.

Friends, my story wouldn't be complete without my thorns. I probably wouldn't tell you about the crossroads I've been through if I didn't have the scars reminding me of where I have been. They are beautiful, and they are a part of who I am today: a God-fearing Jesus-loving girl, who wants nothing more than to share it all with other women. We serve a good God, who has a plan for each one of us. What an epiphany it was when I finally realized that those thorns are there for His reason and for His plan.

Instead of us feeling sorry for ourselves about the life that's been given to us, let's look at it differently. Let's look at it like He looks at it. He wants you to use your thorns for His glory and to grow the Kingdom.

Are you allowing the enemy or God to use your thorns?

I know, I know, it can be scary and overwhelming to think about, because some of us have some ugly thorns, but let's dream for a minute. What if you share about your eating disorder (or your sexual abuse or your depression) and that helps another person come to know Christ, or helps them find strength in their thorn? What if we stopped praying for God to take our thorns, and allowed Him to use them? What if we let His strength shine through our weakness? Remember, he says, "My power works best in weakness."[4]

During my past few years in ministry, I've had opportunities to speak and to share my story. I am not a writer, a speaker, nor am I a Bible scholar, but God has made me capable of doing His work. He has enabled me to get up and share about my thorns and to be real and raw about my past. There are times that I speak and walk off stage thinking, where did that come from? That was not in my notes. I have no doubt He is with me, and knowing that gives me the courage to face hundreds of people so that I can share about the love and forgiveness that God has poured over me.

Now, He hasn't taken away my sweat issue. I know, too much information, but it's true. I sweat mainly under my right armpit and I'm not sure why. Rather than exasperate the problem by fretting, I have finally come to the point of laughing at myself. It has become a joke between friends and family and now all of you. Hopefully one day He will take that away! In the meantime, please laugh along with me (and not at me).

Now back to my point. We must visualize our thorns positively, even though they can be painful. We must see them as purposeful. Don't pray for God to take them away, pray that He will use them! That shift in thought might make a world of difference. I challenge you to memorize 2 Corinthians 12:8-9 and make it your motto!

---

[1] *Life Application Study Bible (NLT)*, Introduction to 2 Corinthians
[2] *Life Application Study Bible (NLT)*, Introduction to 2 Corinthians
[3] *Life Application Study Bible (NLT)*, Commentary on 2 Corinthians 12:2-3
[4] 2 Corinthians 12:9

CHAPTER TWO

# IN THE BEGINNING

I was born and raised in Alabama. I say y'all a lot, I have a hard Southern accent, I love decaf sweet tea and coffee with French vanilla creamer (thank you, Coffee mate®, for contributing to my addiction). My family and I are Auburn fans. War Eagle! I love my family. My husband and I have four kiddos ranging in age from seven to nineteen, and two dogs. Yes, my life is crazy and chaotic, but I have come to realize that this is the season He has me in. I try to embrace it (*try* being the keyword). My family is loud, and I worry that we scare those around us, but we love well. I wouldn't change anything about right now, other than I wish time would slow down a bit!

I also love my quiet time. I didn't come to know Christ until later in my twenties, so I have a passion for transforming my daily life for Him. I'll admit that I completely fail at this most days, but I'm a work in progress. After years of praying and procrastinating, I knew it was time for me to write my story. It has helped me grow in my faith and I hope to encourage readers to grow in their faith. I want to be transparent and real about what my life has looked like—the good, the bad and the ugly.

"For I know the plans I have for you," declares the Lord, "plans to prosper you and not to harm you, plans to give you hope and a future" (Jeremiah 29:11). My plans for life didn't have anything to do with the ministry. Looking back, I'm not sure if I ever had a chance to plan for my future. My life has been a whirlwind of chaos; I was just trying to survive.

I did not grow up in what people would say is a "typical home." I was born in 1980 in Birmingham, Alabama. Shortly after my arrival, my parents divorced. They were both very young and already had one child. My sister may have memories of what our home life was like at that time, but that is not my story to tell. What I remember and know to be true is that my parents divorced for some reason, and to this day, I am not sure why. I have asked but have never gotten a clear answer from either of them. I love my parents but have always felt like they tried to blame the other for whatever happened. Either way, they divorced and went their separate ways. Both remarried several years later. I lived with my mother and stepfather during my childhood years, and my memories began when we moved to a town called Altoona in Alabama. Altoona is probably one of the smallest cities in the state. The population is around 900. I remember when the only traffic light in town was removed because there wasn't enough traffic!

We didn't live in town, however. My parents preferred to be out in the country where there were no neighbors for miles. It was beautiful. We lived on fifty acres of fields, ponds, and barns. I have many good memories of riding four-wheelers, bailing hay, and feeding our many animals. Several years of life passed on the farm before my parents decided to have another child. My beautiful little sister was born on December 5, 1986. Her homecoming was a happy and exciting time! She was a sweet baby and soon became the princess of our family. Meanwhile, I started kindergarten at West End Elementary School. My mother cared for us and our home while my stepdad worked with his parents at his family's printing company in Birmingham.

Preschool

There were times in my childhood when we were active in a Methodist church. I remember my parents talking about how good life was when we were in church (and when they were tithing). Growing up, I learned a little about God but had no relationship with Him. I attended Vacation Bible School some summers and watched Gospel Bill with the other kids, but I never really understood what it was all about. However, I have fond memories of this church. It was where I first sang publicly. I remember a sweet lady practicing with me in front of a cassette player for hours. On the morning of my debut, I was nervous as could be (probably sweating then too), but I managed to stand up and sing "The Blood-Bought Church."

There were members of the church who impacted our family in a big way. These individuals cared for my parents through hard times. I noticed the way these adults loved their families and their church family. I looked up to those Christians and hoped that our family would one day be like that. Their joy was both mysterious and intriguing to me.

Just recently, at one of our women's conferences, I was able to reconnect with several of the families who attended that church. What sweet relationships they have become! They are now prayer partners and encouragers, and I am blessed that God brought them back into my life.

During my elementary years, every other weekend, I would see my father and his wife in Birmingham. They had a son who was a year older than me (adopted from Korea) and a little girl who was born in 1984. My memories of these weekends are all good. We had a beautiful home and friends that lived on the same street. My brother and I would wake up, eat breakfast, and spend all day outside, riding bikes and making forts in the woods across the street from our house. We would have lemonade stands and go to church on Sundays, where I would sit in between my precious grandmother and grandfather at Eastlake Methodist Church and stare at the beautiful stained glass windows that lined the sanctuary. We would take two-week Florida vacations during the summer and spend all day on the beach and in the arcades. I'm sure there were arguments, and I'm sure I got in trouble, but most of our time together was good. I loved being with them, especially my grandparents. When I spent the night with my grandparents, my grandfather (Pop) would make me pancakes and hot tea every morning. My grandmother (Mom) would sit and play hymns at her organ each Saturday night. We watched Disney movies and Braves baseball every weekend.

At my mother and stepfather's farm, we had many animals—goats, cows, pigs, and chickens. I enjoyed feeding and gathering eggs each day. We had two horses, Jack and Jill. In the spring of 1987, my parents were looking to purchase another horse for barrel racing, so one afternoon we went to visit a horse breeder in Oneonta, Alabama. He brought a large horse out for us to look at. He saddled the horse and led him into the corral. Once in, he walked several laps around the corral with the horse, and then my mother mounted the horse to ride. After several minutes, the horse's trot became a fast gallop, and all of a sudden, it broke into a run. My older sister and I stood beside our baby sister in the stroller and watched in horror. We could hear the fear in our mother's voice as she screamed for the horse to stop. My stepfather and the trainer were now in the corral, trying to help. It felt like forever, but within seconds the horse threw my mother off and then proceeded to run over her.

I can't remember much after that; we were definitely in shock. My mother was now lying lifeless in front of us, having a *grand mal* seizure, and bleeding from her ears and nose. Doctors estimated that she hit the ground at 35 miles per hour. She was transported by air to UAB Hospital in a coma with three skull fractures. The medical staff would not let us in her room, though I was able to peek in. I remember her being gray in color and her head was swollen. Family members were there and cried with us when the doctors warned that my mom may not make it. Thankfully, Mother did come out of the coma, and after several weeks, she was able to go home. Sadly, my remaining childhood memories after this event are not as pleasant as the ones before.

Life changed after the accident for all of us. Mother encountered subsequent seizures from the fall, depression, anxiety attacks, memory lapses, and hearing loss. My stepfather continued to commute to Birmingham for work. As a child, I didn't know what to do or think. I found it difficult to talk to my parents—to communicate what I was feeling. Therefore, I kept it all inside. I hid the pain and confusion from everyone. I had one friend whom I trusted; her name was Jana. I felt safe with her family, so I tried to stay at their house as much as possible. I feel like they probably knew there was some dysfunction happening in my home, but they never mentioned it and always welcomed me.

My family eventually stopped going to church. Looking back, the stress of the situation provided easy access for the enemy to creep into our home and create chaos. I noticed my parents changing. They began going out more. It was as if they began relying on themselves and the comforts of this world instead of Christ.

Doubly difficult for me was the fact that I wasn't seeing my biological father as much. Our weekend visits were slowly waning, and I didn't know why. There would always be a reason I couldn't go, or he couldn't come to get me. Then one day, I received news that my father and stepmother were going to divorce. I was devastated. And so hurt. I couldn't understand it because I didn't see it coming. Life was good in their home when I was there. Was that a facade? My hurt turned into anger. As a child, I had no clue how to process this. They divorced, and shortly after, there was a noticeable change in my father. I no longer went to his house regularly, and hardly heard from him. I rarely got to speak to my now ex-stepmother or see my siblings. My visits with Mom and Pop also came to an end.

Several months later, my mother sat down with my older sister and me to let us know that my father had moved to Florida and that we would no longer be seeing him. I know as an adult now there was probably a lot more to the situation than I knew, but the pain of hearing my father up and left (without saying goodbye) stung. I remember sitting on the side of my mother's bed, crying as she told us. Why would my father not want to be my father? I know now that that wasn't the case, but it felt like it from my young perspective. I look back and see the enemy planting more seeds of fear, as well as feelings of unworthiness and abandonment in my mind.

My father and I eventually reconnected, but our relationship wasn't the same. I was able to visit him several times while he lived in Florida, but subsequent communication never lasted long. He had started a new life with a new family.

My home life continued to spiral downward. My family became more distant, each of us struggling with sin and heartache. Over the next several years, we went through hard times financially, spiritually, and mentally. Like I said before, I truly believe the enemy took advantage of our weak state after my mother's accident and used it to destroy our family. We weren't going to church, my parents now drank heavily and were out more than at home. My sister was getting ready to graduate and move away. I was not looking forward to this. As much as we drove each other crazy, my older sister's presence gave me strength. Her departure for college was another loss.

CHAPTER THREE

# WHICH WAY?

In 1994, my brother Adam was killed in a motorcycle accident after school. As he rode down a street, a classmate backed her car out of her driveway and hit him. Because of the way you sit on this type of motorcycle, it tore the arteries away from his heart, and he immediately passed. I was broken. Adam was a good guy; his smile would light up a room! Again, I couldn't process why. The last memory I have of him is us at the beach, listening to a Bush CD that I loved. We listened to it every day of that vacation and sang at the top of our lungs. I stayed at the beach several days after he left, and found the CD tucked into my suitcase with a note written on it, "From: Adam." I still have it. I miss him and often think about what our relationship would be like if he were still alive.

By age fourteen, I had kept my pain and sadness inside for so long it was taking a toll on me mentally. I struggled with self-confidence issues and my desire to be accepted. Coupled with the fact that I was going through the awkward not-so-cute middle school years didn't help matters. Looking back now, I can see that God placed people in my life in certain seasons. In elementary school, it was Mrs. Spears, a sweet lady who worked in the front office. In high school, it was Mrs. Butts. I hope these women know how much I appreciated their help. I won't forget them or how their compassion impacted me. They loved me when I felt no one else did, without questions or judgment.

By high school, my home life was miserable. I dreaded going home because there was always an argument happening. I tried to stay busy with sports and school functions. At this point, my parents' choices were affecting all of us. There were nights I would not see them come home, and mornings that I would be leaving to catch the bus as they were pulling in the driveway (after a long night out with friends). If they came home earlier than dawn, I would often be kept awake by their arguments, worrying about what would happen next.

Thankfully, my sisters and I spent many nights with my grandmother. She was a constant blessing. I remember playing with her makeup and trying on her clothes while the music of John Philip Sousa spun on her record player. She would make us pancakes every morning and take us to Noccalula Falls Park to play. My grandmother was a beautiful woman with a beautiful heart.

My older sister had moved away to college now, and I frequently found myself alone. At the age of thirteen (before my brother died), I started drinking and smoked my first joint of marijuana. It was easy to get into my parents' liquor cabinet and take whatever I wanted. I remember helping myself to whatever bottle I could find, usually vodka, to numb the heartache I felt inside. In front of others, I tried to act like everything was good at home, but that was far from the truth. Things were going on in my house that I didn't want anyone to know about. This pattern continued for several years, leading me into a deep depression.

During my junior year, I was cheering for my high school and making good grades, but still felt miserable inside. I was drinking whenever I had an opportunity and smoking regularly. That February, my stepfather took a position with a company in Georgia, which meant I had to leave everything I had ever known in the middle of a school year. Our new town was lovely but fitting in at school was difficult. My high school in Alabama had had a couple hundred students. I now found myself surrounded by a couple thousand. The kids there all seemingly wore name-brand clothes and drove expensive cars. In the halls, mean girls would make fun of me daily. I felt lost and very alone there at first.

Junior Year

Despite a few nice classmates in Georgia who helped me adjust, I eventually found myself mixing with more popular kids. They were a bad influence, and I knew better. But, in my mind, it was worth the risk because I finally felt like I was fitting in. These kids all came from wealthy families and had access to money and drugs. Having no relationship with God at the time, I wasn't strong enough to say "no" to the temptations. I continued to drink, smoke, and experiment with harder drugs.

At home, my parents were still making poor decisions themselves, so our relationship continued to crumble. Our fights would start with a small disagreement, then yelling would ensue, and someone would eventually make their point by throwing something. After almost a year of this craziness, I decided to leave. I waited until my parents went out one night, packed a bag, and left.

I had nowhere to go but knew I had to get out of the house. As a friend picked me up that night, I remember asking myself if running away was the right decision. I knew it wasn't, but I was hurt and couldn't continue living the way we were. The following few days were very hard. My parents went to the school and told them I was now living out of the district. I was called into the office and asked to turn in my books. Looking back, I don't think that is what my parents intended to happen. Perhaps someone thought that tactic might scare me into coming home. But I was determined to move forward by myself.

I found a job so I could buy food and other necessities and spent nights with various friends (even sleeping in their cars). Planning to finish high school, I managed to find transportation to night classes. It was stressful, but I started to feel more in control of my life. That is until one sunny day when darkness blindsided me yet again.

I remember the weather was wonderful. It was a great day to be outside and I was with a friend who had been letting me stay on his couch. He was driving and we picked up another friend from the restaurant where he worked. We proceeded to turn out of the parking lot, and that's the last thing I remember before I awoke in agonizing pain. Doctors were all around me. The pain in my left leg was especially excruciating. I drifted in and out of consciousness, but I recall people crying. I heard them asking me questions, but I couldn't communicate. All I could do was lay there, as I tried to wrap my head around where I was and what had happened.

I found out later that a van had broadsided our car. I was sitting in the back seat when the impact broke my seatbelt and pushed me under the front seat. I was told that no one knew I was in the car until a lady who saw the accident happen looked in and noticed my hair laying on the seat. The Jaws of Life tool had to be used to cut me out of the car. Paramedics reported that I was not breathing when they initially reached me. I had a concussion and there were contusions on my face, head, and arms that needed stitches. My knee had been crushed and my femur, jaw, and several ribs were broken.

I went through multiple surgeries before leaving the hospital. To this day, I am still scheduling surgeries to repair the resulting damage in my hip and femur. After the car crash I wasn't able to walk, so I attempted to move back in with my parents. I became extremely depressed. Circumstances there were the same. I felt like I had no one to turn to and nowhere to go, but I left anyway, as soon as I could.

I found a female roommate; she and my boyfriend at the time were both drug users. I would come home to prescription pills, marijuana, cocaine, and other drugs lined up on the coffee table. I felt like there was no escaping it. Yet one morning, I woke up and knew things needed to change.

I had no money, no relationship with either set of my parents, and no real friends to turn to for help. I called my older sister, who told me I could stay with her until I found a more permanent place. I left Georgia that day with one bag and the clothes on my back. God was waiting to guide me when I came to the crossroad that led me out of that dark place. I never went back.

After several weeks with my sister, my aunt and uncle graciously took me in. It was a relief to have someone welcome me into their home. I always secretly wanted to live with this family (my father's sister) but never dreamed that would happen. For the first time, I felt genuinely accepted. I had a family who loved me despite my past, and who wanted to be with me. I attended church with them on Sundays. They made God their first priority, and it showed by the way they lived. I was able to go back to high school and finish my senior year. My father slowly came back into my life. I began to see him again and rebuild our relationship. It was wonderful! God was at work.

Senior Portrait

CHAPTER FOUR

# NOT AGAIN

My senior year in high school was great. I was able to be a teenager, without worrying about where I was going to sleep, or what I was going to eat that day. I met friends who accepted me despite my past, and I am still in touch with many of them. My aunt and uncle provided a safe and healthy home for me. I felt loved, accepted, and extremely blessed!

That year I met a nice guy who was several years older than me. He was not from the area but owned a local sign company. After hanging out for several months, we started dating. His family was kind and graciously welcomed me into their circle. We had a wonderful time together riding in his car on back roads, listening to music, or just spending time on the back porch. I graduated in the spring of 1999 and started studying at the local junior college in September. That fall, I found out I was pregnant. Although I struggled with my decision to keep the baby, I knew it was the right thing to do. There was no other option in my mind than to be a mother to this sweet child. Life at that point started to become stressful. I was pregnant; he was working to grow the business. We were kids trying to make it in the real world. But that doesn't excuse the next part of my story.

When I said we had a wonderful time together, we did, but I began to see a pattern in his behavior when he drank too much. There would come a point during our good time when I knew he had consumed enough. If he kept drinking, things could change within seconds. We would be out, either with friends or just the two of us, and I would look in his eyes and know he had crossed that line. His mood would suddenly shift from fun-loving to angry. He would look for a fight, and it would take everything I had to stop him from starting one. I didn't understand where his anger came from and made excuses for it.

But one night, when I was five months pregnant, he came home and abused me for the first time. When he walked through our back door, I knew by the look in his eyes what was about to happen. The next day, he apologized and promised it would never happen again. He had an excuse, and my young, insecure self bought into it. I loved him despite not understanding his behavior.

Most of the time, life was good, but there were times when he would become abusive. Time after time, I would take our child and leave, only to return after he apologized.

I usually turned to his family for support and help. They were very sympathetic and loving. His sister continues to be like a sister to me; I'm so thankful for her. I could not have asked for a more beautiful soul to walk with me through those years. His parents were also supportive during the difficulties and continue to be there for me if needed.

My best friend Kasey witnessed much of this turmoil and the impact alcohol had on my home life. I confided in her, and she would cry with me after incidents happened as we tried to figure out what to do. In full disclosure, I made my share of mistakes in the marriage too. I should have handled certain things differently. After three years of this cycle, his temper flared one night in a drastic way.

My three-year-old son and I were home watching TV and playing. My husband had met friends that day to ride dirt bikes, and they went out to eat afterward. He caught a ride home, and as soon as the door closed, I knew what was about to happen. I don't recall what set him off, but I remember screaming at my son to get upstairs as my husband flipped the chair that my boy and I were sitting in.

I remember seeing the fear and pain in my son's eyes as he watched from the staircase, his father destroying our townhome and my heart. I remember being thrown up against a wall and wishing a neighbor would hear and come save us, but no one responded. I eventually got my husband out of the house and locked the door. That night, I vowed not to allow the abuse to continue. I didn't want my son witnessing something like that again. *Why can't we hold on to the love that brought us together?* I sadly thought. I felt I had no choice but to protect my son and leave my husband. This time, I left for good. It was one of the hardest things I've ever had to do. The worst thing about that night is that to this day, my son remembers everything.

The next couple of years were hard. We suffered through an emotional divorce and many difficult days. I was working, but the money was barely enough to pay my bills and put food on the table for my son and myself. I couldn't afford childcare. Again, I found myself alone and desperately wanting to be loved and wanted. I tried to put my life back together but felt like I was getting nowhere. I came to another crossroad and found myself on the wrong path yet again.

My depression at this point became overwhelming; I was barely able to function. There were days I couldn't get out of bed. I cried myself to sleep and woke up fighting back more tears. I tried to numb the pain with alcohol.

Meanwhile, a friend and coworker introduced me to her neighbors one night. I was not looking for a relationship but found myself intrigued by this one man, Ryan. He was a bit quiet, unlike me. He was also a hard worker, went to church, prayed, and talked openly about his faith. I was so far from God; I had no clue how to communicate with him. But God had him there for a reason.

After several months, he invited me to church. That first Sunday might have been the scariest moment of my life. There I was, a divorced mom walking into this big church where his father was the associate pastor, and his mother was his Sunday School teacher. What a potential disaster! I sat in Sunday School thinking, please don't call on me to read anything or answer any questions about the Bible.

I'm going to apologize to my mother-in-law for publicly telling this story, but it's so funny and to this day, makes our family laugh. After the service ended, Ryan and I walked to find his parents so he could introduce me. We saw his mother and made our way over to her. His mother walked up to me, and before he could introduce me or say anything, she said, "Oh, this is _____ (someone else)?" He said, "No, Mom, this is Cheryl." Her face reddened, and she apologized profusely, but it was a much-needed ice breaker for me. We laughed, and I think she even cried a little bit, bless her heart.

I went to church every Sunday and listened to the Word of God speak to me. I was convicted of so many things and recall being on my knees, praying for help to straighten out my crazy upside-down life. I remember joining Ryan at his parents' house for family dinner. Before each meal, they would pray, which was unusual to me. His mom would say, "Yes, yes," as someone prayed, which startled me at first. Why would someone keep talking out loud during a prayer? I would peek out one eye to figure out who she was talking too, and if she was okay.

I started attending a women's Bible study and participated in events at church. I knew nothing about the Bible and didn't know how to go about reading it, but God kept nudging me to walk with Him. I started to feel a sense of security and belonging, things I had never felt before.

One day on a road trip, I listened to the study "Anointed, Transformed, Redeemed" with Kay Arthur, Beth Moore, and Priscilla Shirer.[1] I listened intently as the women testified about how God had rescued them. I was so convicted and moved by the Holy Spirit, that I sat there in the driver's seat and cried. That night, I continued to cry in bed. One word I had heard that day kept going through my mind, "Crossroads." I sat in bed and started listing all the crossroads I had been through in my life. I then recounted when I chose to take the wrong path. I began to see a pattern. I didn't know it because I didn't have a relationship with him, but God had been with me at those crossroads. That evening, I dropped to my knees once again, praying, crying, and begging for forgiveness.

I went home the next day and immediately called my pastor. I sat in his office and cried uncontrollably (and let me tell you, I have an ugly cry). It was bad! I told our pastor, "I don't know what it's like when God speaks to you, but this just happened." I confessed my convictions to him and told him everything that had been on my heart the night before. His response was, "He's telling you to share your story. You must share your story." My response was, "No, Pastor, I don't speak, I don't write, and I don't tell stories."

Friends, a word of advice: Don't ever tell God, "No." I guarantee you will be convicted, and God's calling will be on your mind so much that you won't eat or sleep. You will eventually drive yourself crazy because you know what you need to do.

---

[1] Kay Arthur, Beth Moore, and Priscilla Shirer, *Anointed, Transformed, Redeemed: A Study of David* (Nashville: LifeWay Press, 2008), CD.

CHAPTER FIVE

# I'VE BEEN WAITING ON YOU

Several weeks later, at church, I felt called to make it public that I had accepted Christ as my personal Savior. I remember jumping up from the pew, no one knowing what I was doing (I'm not sure if I even knew) and heading down to the front. I walked up to our pastor, and his words were, "I have been waiting on you." Those words still weigh on me because I know God was thinking the same thing. He probably says those words to each of us every single day. "I have been waiting on you!"

I can identify with the Samaritan woman by the well in the following passage:

> *Jesus Talks with a Samaritan Woman*
>
> *Now Jesus learned that the Pharisees had heard that he was gaining and baptizing more disciples than John - although, in fact, it was not Jesus who baptized, but his disciples. So he left Judea and went back once more to Galilee. Now he had to go through Samaria. So he came to a town in Samaria called Sychar, near the plot of ground Jacob had given to his son Joseph. Jacob's well was there, and Jesus, tired as he*

*was from the journey, sat down by the well. It was about noon. When a Samaritan woman came to draw water, Jesus said to her, "Will you give me a drink?" (His disciples had gone into the town to buy food.) The Samaritan woman said to him, "You are a Jew, and I am a Samaritan woman. How can you ask me for a drink?" (For Jews do not associate with Samaritans. Jesus answered her, "If you knew the gift of God and who it is that asks you for a drink, you would have asked him, and he would have given you living water.""Sir," the woman said, "you have nothing to draw with, and the well is deep. Where can you get this living water? Are you greater than our father Jacob, who gave us the well and drank from it himself, as did also his sons and his livestock?" Jesus answered, "Everyone who drinks this water will be thirsty again, but whoever drinks the water I give them will never thirst. Indeed, the water I give them will become in them a spring of water welling up to eternal life." The woman said to him, "Sir, give me this water so that I won't get thirsty and have to keep coming here to draw water." He told her, "Go, call your husband, and come back." "I have no husband," she replied. Jesus said to her, "You are right when you say you have no husband. The fact is, you have had five husbands, and the man you now have is not your husband. What you have just said is quite true." "Sir," the woman said, "I can see that you are a prophet. Our ancestors worshiped on this mountain, but you Jews claim that the place where we must worship is in Jerusalem." "Woman," Jesus replied, "believe me, a time is coming when you will worship the Father neither on this mountain nor in Jerusalem. You Samaritans worship what you do not know; we worship what we do know, for salvation is from the Jews. Yet a time is coming and has now come when the true worshipers will worship the Father in the Spirit and in truth, for they are the kind of worshipers the Father seeks. God is spirit, and his worshipers must worship in the Spirit and in truth." The woman said, "I know that Messiah (called Christ) is coming. When he comes, he will explain everything to us." Then Jesus declared, "I, the one speaking to you - I am he." (John 4:1-26)*

*The Disciples Rejoin Jesus*

*Just then his disciples returned and were surprised to find him talking with a woman. But no one asked, "What do you want?" or "Why are you talking with her?" Then, leaving her water jar, the woman went back to the town and said to the people, "Come, see a man who told me everything I ever did. Could this be the Messiah?" They came out of the town and made their way toward him. Meanwhile his disciples urged him, "Rabbi, eat something." But he said to them, "I have food to eat that you know nothing about." Then his disciples said to each other, "Could someone have brought him food?" "My food," said Jesus, "is to do the will of him who sent me and to finish his work. Don't you have a saying, 'It's still four months until harvest'? I tell you, open your eyes and look at the fields! They are ripe for harvest. Even now the one who reaps draws a wage and harvests a crop for eternal life, so that the sower and the reaper may be glad together. Thus the saying 'One sows and another reaps' is true. I sent you to reap what you have not worked for. Others have done the hard work, and you have reaped the benefits of their labor." (John 4:27-38)*

*Many Samaritans Believe*

*Many of the Samaritans from that town believed in him because of the woman's testimony, "He told me everything I ever did." So when the Samaritans came to him, they urged him to stay with them, and he stayed two days. And because of his words many more became believers. They said to the woman, "We no longer believe just because of what you said; now we have heard for ourselves, and we know that this man really is the Savior of the world." (John 4:39-42)*

During biblical times women would go and retrieve water each day from a well. This was the highlight of their day, because it was a chance to chat with other women. Since sin was already in the world, I suspect there was some gossip going on. I imagine just as Southern women word it, the Samaritan women would start a sentence with, "I don't mean to gossip, but ..." or they may have ended a conversation with, "Bless her heart." Either way, we can be confident that rumors circulated as these women filled their water containers. Knowing what we know about the woman in John 4, she was probably the topic of conversation repeatedly being she was an outcast with a scandalous past. She had been married five times and now lived with a new man. The town wanted nothing to do with her, and therefore she would retrieve her water at a different time than others. She even went to a well where presumably fewer people gathered.

When she arrived at Jacob's well on this documented day, who was there? JESUS. I get so excited thinking about it! Jesus was there at the well waiting on her. He knew she was coming, and He chose her (of all people) to be part of the setting where He first reveals his true identity as the Messiah. Defying racial division and gender taboos, Jesus asked the woman for a drink from her water container. He demonstrated his divinity by telling the woman about her life. She innately responded by telling the townspeople that she had met the Messiah. She led them back to Jesus, and as a result, many more believed that He was who He claimed to be. Even though she typically tried to avoid her neighbors, she shared her story because she knew she was privy to incredible knowledge that must not be kept secret.[1]

I LOVE THIS! I, too, have been an outcast. I'm sure there are people from my past that question me being in ministry. But I'm okay with that. I want to run into every town I can, proclaiming what He has done, how he was waiting on me, and how He has redeemed me. We can learn much from this woman's example.

How can you share your spiritual experiences with others?

God waited on me for more than twenty years to turn to Him for help and guidance. I finally prayed and accepted Him as Lord of my life and was baptized on Mother's Day of 2005. Immediately, I knew that God had a plan for me (He has a plan for each of us). The crossroads in my life became more comfortable to maneuver through, and I could now sense which path to take.

I still find it hard to believe that He wants me as a daughter after all those years of disobedience. His love is a love I have never been shown before, a love that is incomprehensible, rewarding, and promising. I want more of Him. I can't know Him enough.

Is He still waiting on you?

---

[1] John MacArthur, *Twelve Extraordinary Women* (Nashville: Thomas Nelson, 2005), 141-154.

CHAPTER SIX

# BUT, GOD?

Ryan and I continued to grow in Christ together through our dating years. I felt like I could be myself with Ryan. Life was comfortable. He made me feel loved and wanted, yet was respectful to both Timothy and me (which made me love him even more). We married in April of 2007. It was a beautiful traditional Baptist wedding, and my son walked me down the aisle. Kasey, my longtime friend, stood by my side. She later became my sister-in-law when she married Ryan's brother, and is known as Aunt KK to our children. Our first pastor came back to marry Ryan and me. During the ceremony before our vows, the pastor gave me a white Bible, a gracious gift from Ryan's parents, my soon-to-be in-laws.

The pastor directed Ryan and me to hold the Bible together in our hands as we vowed, "With this Bible, we will bring our lives together before Christ and base it around God's Word." I put this precious Bible in our china cabinet, where I see it daily. It's something I will cherish forever!

Ryan and I have a good marriage and have been blessed with three more children; however, I regret not remembering our vows more often through the years. All marriages have their ups and downs, and everyone struggles with insecurities. Be aware that the enemy can creep into daily routine and use those insecurities to plant seeds of doubt and frustration within a marriage and other relationships. I don't want to give the enemy credit for anything, but he wants nothing more than to destroy people and families. The next time you or I come to a relational crossroad, let's promise, "With this Bible, we will bring our lives together before Christ and base it around God's Word."

"The thief comes only to steal and kill and destroy; I have come that they may have life, and have it to the full" (John 10:10).

Ryan and Timothy at our wedding

Recently I was asked to speak at a youth event. The leaders wanted me to share my story and pick a woman in the Bible with whom I could relate. I immediately thought of Martha. Confession time: How many of us stand in our kitchen or fold laundry while staring at our family thinking, *Sure, I will cook dinner (or fold clothes) while you sit there and watch TV!* I imagine most of us can relate to Martha.

"As Jesus and the disciples continued on their way to Jerusalem, they came to a certain village where a woman named Martha welcomed him into her home. Her sister, Mary, sat at the Lord's feet, listening to what he taught. But Martha was distracted by the big dinner she was preparing. She came to Jesus and said, "Lord, doesn't it seem unfair to you that my sister just sits here while I do all the work? Tell her to come and help me" (Luke 10:38-42).

We have all been there. The crazy thing is, I love cooking and serving people, but my ugly deceitful heart will get the best of me sometimes. I'm left standing in my kitchen, feeling frustrated, much like Martha. She watched from her kitchen as Mary sat at Jesus's feet, annoyed and angry that she couldn't be in there doing the same thing. But Jesus makes a point in saying all these roles are essential. The difference is where our heart is in serving. Are we serving with a pure heart or a selfish heart? And my family, we were stepping into a new season with wonderful opportunities that can only be from Him. But we were stepping into a time where my heart struggled with these roles of wife, mother, and leader.

After several years of marriage, my husband's job brought us to Owensboro, Kentucky. It was an excellent opportunity for him, a two-year contract managing the build of a new hospital; however, we initially thought we were moving to Charleston, South Carolina. You might imagine my reaction when Ryan told me about the change in plans. I think my first words were, "Where the heck is Owensboro, Kentucky?"

Driving to our new town for the first time, I remember exchanging apprehensive looks with my son as we passed barn after barn surrounded by corn and tobacco fields. We were on a road that natives here call "The Natcher." We fondly referred to it as "the never-ending road." Despite our fear of isolation, we were determined to keep our family together and make the best of it, no matter what awaited us.

Once in Owensboro, we found a great neighborhood. Our son was about to start fifth grade. We joined a local church, and then something strange happened. Almost immediately, I felt like God was calling me to pursue a women's ministry position there. I again told God, "No. I can't serve in that area, anything but women. I have no clue how to work with women, never mind the fact that I am a new believer myself. I still have so much more to learn about your Word!" Also, my home life was a hot mess due to the move, Ryan working twelve hours a day, and me being pregnant. I thought, *There is no way I can get into women's ministry right now.*

I think I told you earlier, but don't ever tell God, "No." Time went on, and God kept nudging. I think at one point he pushed, but I will ask Him about that later. I eventually surrendered and called the church. I spoke to our pastor and the acting women's ministry director, and what do you know? The women's director had been praying for someone to come along and take the lead. Hmm, of course, she was!

I accepted the position. From that point forward, God used me in ways I cannot explain. I've confided in my husband on numerous occasions, "I have no clue what I am doing," but God keeps nudging me to take one more step. I'm not a natural leader, especially as it relates to other women. I don't even have a good track record with female friends. I'm not a Bible scholar. And as I mentioned earlier, my right armpit sweats. Also, my neck and ears turn red when I have to speak in front of people. Isn't that weird? That's why I kept saying, "But God? But God? But God, why me?"

I went to a women's conference soon after and was overwhelmed by God's presence there. I knew then I had to stop second-guessing Him. It was time to walk in faith and trust in the Father wholeheartedly.

One of my first events at church was a big dinner for the women in our community. Providentially, we were able to schedule Jennie Allen (Bible teacher, author, and founder of IF:Gathering) as our speaker. While driving her from the airport to our venue, I made a request. We wanted to designate a time for the women to write down their prayer requests and place the papers under a cross on the stage. This symbolized each woman casting their cares upon the Father. She obliged, and after her talk the women did that, and we prayed over the requests before dismissing for the night.

Afterward, I took the papers home and read through them to see how I could help our women. They were not signed; each request was anonymous. I cried as I repeatedly read words of brokenness. Christian women, believers, mothers, daughters, grandmothers—these 300 women were hurting. Reading the cards, I pictured myself at their crossroads, and I empathized with their loss of hope. I was familiar with their pain, having experienced similar circumstances before coming to know Christ. I was troubled by the fact that many of the women who were sad and struggling were believers.

These cards remained on my mind as I continued to walk in faith. I thought, *If we as Christians and believers are failing to come alongside each other during trials, how can we as a body capably reach unbelievers and the unchurched?*

We must each be spiritually healthy to spread the Good News. If our relationship with God is on shaky ground, we will hesitate to share hope with those who seek it. The enemy will use our thorns to numb us to the needs of others and to keep us in our comfort zones. That makes me uneasy, just thinking about it. Don't be held back by the enemy. Pursue peace of mind through your relationship with God, so that he can use you for eternal purposes.

Sharing my story and encouraging others to do the same has become a passion. Not only should we share our story, but we should confidently claim them! Sisters, we all have a story. Whether it is a lovely account of knowing Him since childhood or a tragic tale of redemption and restoration, it's your God-given story to share so others can be encouraged. Relating to each other is how friendships are formed. I wish we had time to sit down for coffee (with French vanilla creamer) and swap stories. Don't doubt the power of your testimony and how it can influence and inspire those with whom you share.

I later began to see God moving in our women at church—older members taking new steps in faith to build deeper relationships with God and others, women accepting Jesus as their Savior, brave ladies sharing their stories for the first time, and others finding joy in their everyday lives. These women are on fire for Him, and it's been inspiring to me! Working as a women's ministry director was an incredible season in my life, but after several years in that role, God again tested my faith with a new assignment.

This time, I didn't say no (that lesson has been learned). I felt God calling me to create a ministry that would reach women from all generations, denominations, races, and backgrounds. I envisioned various groups of women coming together to worship and grow our Savior's kingdom. Thus began the tedious task of completing legal paperwork to found an organization called Connecting Ministries. In 2016, we received our non-profit approval. Resigning from my position at church was bittersweet. I was sad and scared but also excited. God has been faithful every step since.

It's now 2020, and I am in awe of how God has moved this past year, despite logistical setbacks, financial worries, and showdowns with the enemy. We have seen God provide the very day we needed money to pay for a speaker deposit, and we have seen Him move in the lives and hearts of women all over the country. The Connecting Ministries story continues to unfold, and it gives me chills writing about it. It's a God thing, He is incredible, and I will forever praise Him for using me, thorns and all.

CHAPTER SEVEN

# CROSSROADS

Let's talk about crossroads. Everyone encounters them on life's road, both believers and non-believers. When we arrive at a crossing, we must discern which path to take. In Jeremiah 6:16, the Lord says, "Stop at the crossroads and look around. Ask for the old, godly way, and walk in it. Travel its path, and you will find rest for your souls. But you reply, 'No, that's not the road we want!'"

Just like Jeremiah's audience (the people of Judah circa 600 BC) we also tend to follow the easiest path. We naturally avoid challenging or bumpy roads if we can help it. But God has never promised believers that our walk would be easy. "You can enter God's kingdom only through the narrow gate. The highway to hell is broad, and its gate is wide for the many who choose that way. But the gateway to life is very narrow and the road is difficult, and only a few ever find it" (Matthew 7:13-14).

Visualize that verse. The broad highway to hell is chosen by many because it's enticing. I definitely ran with the pack on that big paved road before knowing Christ. Highways have been cleared of obstacles and bumps and are easy to move through. The alternative path to God's kingdom is unpaved and more difficult. It sounds like we need God's help even to find it. But I can say from experience that I felt lost, alone, and hurt on the enemy's enticing road. Now that I have found the gateway to life, I know I'm not traveling alone. I can rely on God for guidance and strength when the path grows narrow and hilly.

Looking back at my life, I can recall the crossroads I have faced. People question my story, and some kindly express pity about where I have been, but it's okay. I know God causes everything to work together for the good of those who love Him; therefore, I don't question why I went through the things I did.[1] I know the truth, and the truth is that we have a loving, merciful God who desires for us to know Him. He waited on me at various crossroads for many years. He wanted me to choose His path, but I didn't see it. Now I know the hope that He provides to followers who believe in Him and who seek to find the narrow gate.

## REFLECTION ONE + CROSSROAD EXAMINATION

Think about the crossroads in your life to date or the path you are on right now. List them in the space below (past and present). For example, particular decisions about friends, free time, education, dating relationships, employment, marriage, family, career or ministry that you feel have shaped your story.




Did you rely on God during these times? Are you seeking His guidance through present day circumstances? Note scripture or people that He placed in your life for these seasons.

If you answered *no* to the above question, how did you or are you maneuvering through the crossroad or situation? Are you solely self-reliant or have you consulted other people for advice?




How can you seek guidance from God the Father, God the Son, and God the Holy Spirit moving forward?




"Trust in the Lord with all your heart; do not depend on your own understanding. Seek his will in all you do, and he will show you which path to take" (Proverbs 3:5-6). God's Word assures us that He will be with us and guide us throughout life. Trust Him with all of your heart, and He will show you which path to take at the next crossroad. "Your word is a lamp to guide my feet and a light for my path" (Psalm 119:105).

---

[1] Romans 8:28

CHAPTER EIGHT

# SHARING YOUR STORY

Working in ministry, I've met many Christians who are afraid to share their stories because they fear judgment about their past. When we worry about that, we wrestle with the enemy until we are spiritually spent. We are all born lost, many of us have learned lessons the hard way, but by God's grace, our stories of sin and suffering can be used to help others. Ask God to help you overcome that fear of what others may think, so He can begin using your story for His glory.

"Don't you realize that all of you together are the temple of God and that the Spirit of God lives in you?" (1 Corinthians 3:16). We are called to be a unified body of believers. The definition of *unified* is "made uniform or whole; united."[1] As brothers and sisters in Christ, we need to walk with each other instead of tearing each other down. Don't pass judgment or gossip about another's past. I'll admit that I have been guilty of doing so, but I have also been on the receiving end. I know now this is one way the enemy tries to divide and destroy a body of believers.

When I began working in ministry, some people doubted if it was a good fit for me. I felt like certain people probed me with questions because of my past. But I knew that God was calling me to a mission. At the crossroad, I could have listened to the doubts of others or followed the Lord's leading. Thankfully, I made the right decision by choosing to step into ministry. God has affirmed such to me through a sense of His presence. That's not to say I wasn't hesitant and fearful, but friends came alongside to encourage and pray with me, and it helped! Now that I have shared my testimony multiple times, I can tell you with confidence that God will use your story to work in the hearts of others. If it results in God's kingdom growing and believers maturing, then it's worth risking our reputation.

Our life experiences frame the way we see the world. However, as believers in Christ, we are capable of looking around us through His lens of love. After becoming a staff member at church, I saw how some of our women there were hurting. It surprised me because as a fairly new Christ-follower, I assumed that everyone held fast to proverbial pointers like "Turn it over to God," "Cast your cares on Him," and "Put your hope in Him." But that can be easier said than done. As individuals, we deal with distress in different ways, and the support our church family provides can help us apply biblical wisdom through difficult circumstances.

I am a fixer. And yes, I know there are three parts when it comes to God's work: my effort, their responsibility, and the Holy Spirit's influence. But as a body of believers, we are each commanded to come alongside our brothers and sisters in Christ. Let's not forget that. Love others where they are (even if they are on the wrong path) and share truth with them. Being a Christian doesn't make us immune to pitfalls. In fact, the enemy will work hard to turn one's faith around. Throughout my time in women's ministry, I've seen and heard prayer requests regarding addictions (drug, alcohol, pornography, and food), marriage issues, weight issues, self-confidence or worth, anxiety, and depression. I couldn't figure it out. Women who looked as if they had it all together were battling major issues. Women who faithfully attended church every week and volunteered were hurting.

There are women in need of friends everywhere—in church, at work, and among play date groups. She might be your best friend, the woman working as a cashier at the grocery store, or your child's teacher. We are all going through things, and if life is good today, it may not be tomorrow. Women tend to walk around and smile while hiding their true feelings because that's what society implies we need to do. If we slow down, listen, and focus on seeing the world through Jesus's lens of love, we will be able to minister to each other in the way we are called to. "Instead, you must worship Christ as Lord of your life. And if someone asks about your hope as a believer, always be ready to explain it" (1 Peter 3:15).

What keeps us from reaching out? Multiple excuses—we're scared, we're not equipped, we doubt we are strong enough in our faith to walk with someone else, scripture doesn't come to mind, maybe we're battling sin ourselves, and the list goes on. These are examples of us allowing the enemy to use our thorns instead of relying on Christ. Remember, he wants to keep us scared and in our comfort zones! He's continually planting seeds of doubt and reminders of failure in your head to keep you standing still. The devil numbs, but God has overcome. Your sins are forgiven, so don't let them hold you back.

There is no good reason to neglect someone in need. God assures us in scripture that He will be with us, He will go before us, and He will equip us. "Each time he said, 'My grace is all you need. My power works best in weakness.' So now I am glad to boast about my weaknesses, so that the power of Christ can work through me" (2 Corinthians 12:9). "Don't be afraid, for I am with you. Don't be discouraged, for I am your God. I will strengthen you and help you. I will hold you up with my victorious right hand" (Isaiah 41:10).

## REFLECTION TWO + ENCOURAGE A FRIEND

Think about the crossroads in your life. Is there a part of your story that could encourage or equip someone to overcome sin in their life? Think about people you know who may be struggling somehow. How can you relate to them and communicate your empathy? List their names below and plan to call or get together with them.

This life we live is messy, and we need friends in our corner to encourage us. Be that friend to someone else. Cry with them through difficulties and laugh with them when times are good. Stay in the Word so you can share God's truth in various seasons. God has put some amazing women and men in my life who encourage me weekly and even daily. I share that because I believe there are angels on earth for you too. If you belong to a church but do not feel supported right now, pray that God will meet your need. Pray that God would reveal opportunities to connect with those around you, especially those you may be able to advise from experience. Write out your prayer.

---

[1] Lexico, s.v. "unified (a.)," accessed March 23, 2020, https://www.lexico.com/en/definition/unified.

CHAPTER NINE

# WALKING IN FAITH

When Moses, the great Israelite leader, passed away, Joshua stepped forward in faith to succeed him. Due to disobedience and distrust in God, the Israelites had been wandering in the desert for forty years. During that time, God's people faced various crossroads, where they made poor decisions because they lacked faith in God's plan. That generation passed away without seeing the Promised Land. Now the next generation had a chance to get it right. Joshua assured his people that faith and obedience to God would bring them victory. How glorious is that? "This is my command—be strong and courageous! Do not be afraid or discouraged. For the Lord your God is with you wherever you go" (Joshua 1:9).

When I finally made my way to the front of the church to accept Christ, my pastor said, "I have been waiting on you." God patiently waited on me while I wandered through thorns in the desert, taking wrong turn after wrong turn. But friends, remember that our wounds are not worthless. If we have faith in and are obedient to God's Word, we can overcome the past and bring glory to Him. No matter where you are in your walk with the Lord, He is with you. "Do not be afraid or discouraged, for the LORD will personally go ahead of you. He will be with you; he will neither fail you nor abandon you" (Deuteronomy 31:8).

This part of God's story about his people gives me hope because I too wondered for many years (twenty-three years to be exact). Yet He is transforming this broken, sinful girl into someone He can use for a higher purpose. Since I began trusting in the Father's plan, doors have opened before me, and I have seen God at work like I could never have imagined.

In women's ministry at church, I felt God calling me to go deeper. While reading my Bible one day, I came to Hebrews 12:1, "Therefore, since we are surrounded by such a huge crowd of witnesses to the life of faith, let us strip off every weight that slows us down, especially the sin that so easily trips us up. And let us run with endurance the race God has set before us."

I heard God say, "Cheryl, you laid it down. You are forgiven. Now run!" I fell to my knees in prayer and begged Him to equip me and use me for whatever He intended. It was an emotional moment for me. I called my husband afterward in tears, and told him about my encounter with God. He began to pray with me for direction.

I consulted with several mentors who were walking with me during that time. One was my predecessor (and now a dear friend), Mary Martha. I would frequently call her to share prayer requests. Mary Martha and I were watching God move among fellow women at church. It was affirming and inspiring to me. After reading Hebrews 12:1, I was ready to run harder myself! Soon after, I sat with Mary Martha at a table in our preschool area and told her about what God was calling me to do. I was scared.

God was calling me to share my story. Despite my fear of doing that, I intentionally prayed that He would put people in my path for that purpose. I asked Him to equip me to speak to others and to share His Word. And God answered that prayer.

Simultaneously, the enemy tried to discourage me. Doubts and questions continued to run through my mind ... *Who are you? What do you have to say? You're not good enough. You don't even know the books of the Bible.* I was questioned by others about my plans, which terrified me. Imagine thorny walls rising from the ground around my feet, threatening to contain me!

Keeping Hebrews 12:1 in mind, I began running and trusting in His plan. I started believing in the mission God had assigned to me. I listened to encouragers like Mary Martha, who pushed me past insecurities. Again, I felt like I had chosen the right path at a crossroad. God was there, and because I had a relationship with Him, I could see Him. I realized the blinders were gone because my eyes were focused on Jesus. It was a beautiful breakthrough for me spiritually.

I now prayed daily, *God, use me in whatever way you want.* That's when He began to open doors for me to share my story of depression, abuse, and addictions in presentations for local non-profit organizations One evening, I hosted an event at church for the women in shelters and rehabilitation centers. As I stood on stage, my heart hurt as I looked out at their faces. I didn't want them to see me as a woman who had it all together. I wanted them to know about my past, and to know about my current sin and trials. I wanted them to see that it is only through Christ Jesus that I had been able to find my purpose.

I prayerfully continued to host similar events at church and invited other women in our congregation to share their stories. Women between the ages of twenty and eighty left their facades at the door and shared their matter-of-fact stories. The result was wonderful. We noticed personal walls coming down and friendships being built. To this day, those women are turning to each other for support through trials. I share that example to show how one step of faith can move mountains. Are you willing to walk forward and trust in God's plan for you?

The Israelites floundered for forty years before learning this lesson. And then Joshua led his people by faith into the Promised Land. They were victorious at Jericho because they finally believed God when He said that He would give them the land.

Friends, there are people in your church and community who want to run with you. Lock arms and go. Pray intentionally about why He has you where you are. Step forward in faith and allow God to be your strength. Watch Him open doors for you and discover God's purpose for your life!

## REFLECTION THREE + YOUR NEXT STEP

What is God calling you to right now? Do you trust Him? Have you stepped outside of your comfort zone yet to accept your mission? Pray about and plan out your next step, and then take action.

CHAPTER TEN

# FERVENT PRAYER

One of my favorite books in the Bible is Ephesians. Each time I read it, I know I will walk away refreshed and ready for my day, suited up in the armor God gives. In this New Testament book, we find instruction about our daily walk with Christ. Paul wrote this letter to followers of Jesus Christ in Ephesus and opened by praising God for His goodness.

"May God our Father and the Lord Jesus Christ give you grace and peace. All praise to God, the Father of our Lord Jesus Christ, who has blessed us with every spiritual blessing in the heavenly realms because we are united with Christ. Even before he made the world, God loved us and chose us in Christ to be holy and without fault in his eyes" (Ephesians 1:2-4).

How beautiful and encouraging are these words! God chose us in Christ to be holy and without fault. If we confess our sin and ask God for forgiveness through Christ, then God will graciously grant forgiveness, and we will one day be with our Father in heaven.

Friends, He chose you and me! Now we need to align our daily lives with the ways of Christ. Lay your burdens and bad habits at His feet and pick up your cross. Listen for His voice and live out the life He has predestined for you, His chosen one. Allow Him to work in your weaknesses, so His power can be shown to all.

Nine years ago, I walked through a tough time with my family. The circumstances were out of my control, but I was letting the enemy get the best of me. I have explained that my family and I moved to Kentucky, and how it was disappointing in comparison to the prospect of Charleston, South Carolina. So there I was in Owensboro, surrounded by farms and fields, pregnant, with a three-year-old and a fifth grader. I didn't know anyone, and my husband was working twelve hours a day. I probably wasn't the most pleasant person to be around.

I was worn out and irritated. I felt like my husband was putting his job before our family. Because of that, I didn't think he was being the spiritual leader of our home. Once that thorn sprang up, the enemy used anything and everything to fuel my frustrations. I frequently criticized Ryan. "You didn't do this right." "When are you going to do that?" It wasn't pretty.

I was not intentional about my prayer life, and I grew more frustrated because things weren't changing. In fact, it felt like life was getting worse. Our house in Alabama was on the market but not selling. We were blessed with a baby girl, our third child, but she cried all day and all night. I had no time to myself. Moms, you know what I'm talking about. Going to the bathroom or taking a shower felt like an accomplishment. We had no family nearby to call for help. It was horrible.

Our pediatrician lived behind us, and one day I had had all I could take. I looked a mess. No sleep, no shower, and in survival mode, I walked to his house with the baby. His wife, Michelle, answered the door. I gave her the baby and said, "Help." Michelle, in her loving, sweet, and patient voice, said, "Cheryl, go home, take a shower, and take a nap. Let me watch her." I told her, "This baby is crazy! Something must be wrong with her." Later that afternoon, Michelle called me and said, "Hey, you and Ryan get some sleep tonight. Brian and I want to keep her so we can monitor her and see what's going on." Y'all, that was the best night's sleep I have ever had! The next day, Michelle brought our little one home. When she walked in, she smiled and said, "Yep, she's crazy."

And so continued the most exhausting season of life I had ever been through. My baby seemed to be in constant pain, and there was nothing we could do to stop it. I felt sure we were done having kids. That is until I found out we were pregnant again. I sat on the side of our bathtub sobbing to Ryan, "I can't do this again!" Then, God opened my eyes to how the enemy was trying to break me.

God's Spirit laid it on my heart to read Ephesians. I read through it several times, trying to figure out what he wanted me to see or hear through His Word. That week I went to our local Lifeway store, and a five-dollar sale book by the register caught my attention. I picked it up and bought it. (I'm not a reader, so when that happens, it's probably providence.) I didn't look at the back or really register what the title meant, but I went home that day and started reading. I couldn't put it down. You know why? Because it was about the book of Ephesians. God is good!

The book was *Fervent: A Woman's Battle Plan for Serious, Specific, and Strategic Prayer* by Priscilla Shirer. The definition of the word *fervent* is "having or displaying a passionate intensity."[1] I had to read that several times because it made me question my prayer life. During that time, I was searching for structure, guidance, and clarity about my chaotic circumstances. I was praying, but not specifically about the issues that were arising.

Priscilla wrote, "If all we're doing is flinging words and emotions in all directions without any real consideration for the specific ways the enemy is targeting us and the promises of God that apply to us, we're mostly just wasting our time. We're adding to the confusion while not really making a noticeable dent in the problem or the process. We're fighting to keep our heads above water, yet feeling pretty sure on most days we're fighting a losing battle."[2]

Prayer is a powerful gift from God, a way for us to communicate with Him. But like any conversation, it requires focus and thought. God will detect the passion in fervent prayer. Were my prayers fervent nine years ago? Are they fervent today? If the answer is no, that doesn't mean God ignores my prayers. However, I believe the enemy used my aimless prayer life to his advantage. I allowed him to steer my passion away from God, fuel my frustrations, and take away my joy. He was trying to diminish the most powerful tool I have, and that is prayer. The enemy knows that if I toss thoughtless emotions and words up to heaven, that I might arrive at the conclusion that God is not listening when nothing changes. Can you relate? Remember that God is omnipresent. He is almighty and everywhere. When you question where He is or if He is listening, He is by your side, and He can hear you!

After reading *Fervent*, I realized that I was not then praying with intention. Satan is very strategic. Priscilla identifies ten areas in which the enemy targets us.[3] They are our *passion, focus, identity, family, confidence, calling, purity, rest/contentment, heart, and relationships*. I could give an example of how I've struggled in each of these areas. Looking back, I now see that I was under attack.

Friends, the enemy will tear you down any way he can. Be aware of this. One poor decision on my part can send me on a downward spiral fast, and that's precisely where Satan wants me: spinning out of control and away from Christ.

I started thinking about my decisions and the resulting chaos which had crept into my home. This chaos didn't just affect me, it affected my children and my husband. I permitted Satan to feed me feelings of failure instead of arming myself with the Word of God and praying about my frustrations.

Our baby is now a sweet little girl, and people don't believe me when I tell the story, but we do have video footage to prove it! Later, when she had her tonsils taken out, the doctor commented, "Somehow, she already has nodules and damage to her voice box." Yep, that's right. Her dad and I know why.

When we feel the enemy advancing, we need to be in fervent prayer. We need to be passionate about our relationship with Christ and lean on Him through hard times. Paul writes about the armor of God in Ephesians. How many of us wake up and consciously step into this armor? Why wouldn't we? It's there for us to use, and we need to suit up daily to withstand Satan's attacks. Be aware of his targets - your *passion, focus, identity, family, confidence, calling, purity, rest/contentment, heart,* and *relationships.*

### The Whole Armor of God

*A final word: Be strong in the Lord and in his mighty power. Put on all of God's armor so that you will be able to stand firm against all strategies of the devil. For we are not fighting against flesh-and-blood enemies, but against evil rulers and authorities of the unseen world, against mighty powers in this dark world, and against evil spirits in the heavenly places. Therefore, put on every piece of God's armor so you will be able to resist the enemy in the time of evil. Then after the battle you will still be standing firm. Stand your ground, putting on the belt of truth and the body armor of God's righteousness. For shoes, put on the peace that comes from the Good News so that you will be fully prepared. In addition to all of these, hold up the shield of faith to stop the fiery arrows of the devil. Put on salvation as your helmet, and take the sword of the Spirit, which is the word of God. Pray in the Spirit at all times and on every occasion. Stay alert and be persistent in your prayers for all believers everywhere. (Ephesians 6:10-18)*

This passage begins with a warning, "Be strong in the Lord and in his mighty power." To be strong, we need each piece of God's armor. The "belt of truth" is listed first. Jesus said, "I am the way, the truth, and the life. No one can come to the Father except through me" (John 14:6). Believe in Jesus Christ and trust in His message. His words, recorded in the New Testament, are often written in red.

Next is the "body armor of God's righteousness." Picture an armed Roman or Israelite soldier prepared for battle. A typical armed soldier wore a breastplate made of bronze or chain mail. It covered vital organs like the heart and was fitted with loops or buckles that attached it to a thick belt. If the belt was loosened, the breastplate slipped right off.[4] So to protect our hearts, we must firmly believe in the truth of Jesus (our belt).

Shoes allow us to step freely and without fear, so we can pay full attention to the battle at hand. Think about stepping on rock, debris, and thorns. We wouldn't attempt to do that without shoes. If we did, we would have to look down as we walked instead of ahead. Our attention would be diverted, and we wouldn't see the enemy coming. Prepare for each day by putting on shoes: "peace that comes from the Good News." If our minds are at peace, if we are resting in the promises of God, then we will be prepared for whatever lies ahead.

A Roman shield was called a *scutum*. This type of shield was as large as a door and would cover the warrior entirely. Such a shield was not just defensive but could also be used to push opponents. When fighting as a group, soldiers could position their shields to form an enclosure around themselves. This enclosure was called a *testudo,* meaning "tortoise." A testudo was used when advancing upon a city. This tactic protected against flying arrows that were launched from walls above. Shields (often made of wood and then covered in hide) when wet, could extinguish flaming arrows.[5] Our "shield of faith" is powerful like that; it can "stop the fiery arrows of the devil."

As a soldier in Paul's day suited up for battle, a helmet would be the final piece he would put in place. It goes without saying, but without a helmet, a soldier would be so vulnerable that the rest of the armor would be of little use. In Ephesians, "the helmet of salvation" refers to the requirement of salvation through Christ for eternal life. Even if we face death in this life, we will be victorious. Paul said, "For to me, living means living for Christ, and dying is even better" (Philippians 1:21).

The sword used by Roman soldiers was known as a *gladius*. In the hands of a skilled man, it was a fearsome weapon and became known as "the sword that conquered the world." It was sharpened on both sides, making it lethal against an unarmored foe. The point was also sharpened, enabling it to pierce even armor.[6] Paul defines the "sword of the Spirit" as the word of God. The author of Hebrews also makes this reference: "For the word of God is alive and powerful. It is sharper than the sharpest two-edged sword, cutting between soul and spirit" (Hebrews 4:12).

Scripture says, "Put on all of God's armor so that you will be able to stand firm against all strategies of the devil" (Ephesians 6:11). Every morning before your feet hit the floor, pray that God will protect you, your husband, and your children with His armor. Pray the same for your church family. Make this a daily practice.

Paul tells us that in the future we will *become*, but until then, we must *overcome*. "We can rejoice, too, when we run into problems and trials, for we know that they help us develop endurance. And endurance develops strength of character, and character strengthens our confident hope of salvation. And this hope will not lead to disappointment. For we know how dearly God loves us, because he has given us the Holy Spirit to fill our hearts with his love" (Romans 5:3-5).

These passages give me hope. I know that through my trials, God is making and molding me for His purpose. There have been days I didn't want to see anyone, times I would cry all day, and moments when I felt hopeless, but I did overcome. And I will continue to overcome because of the strength He gives me. I am allowing Him to use my thorns for His glory. When I feel the enemy attacking, the first thing I do is go to the One who rescued me! The One who gave up His life so I could have eternal life.

Will you join me in fervently praying for each other and for our families? Let's pray with precision and suit up daily in the armor of God. I like how Priscilla puts it in her book, "Prayer is the portal that brings the power of heaven down to earth."[7]

Timothy, Peyton, Layla, and Mia

## REFLECTION FOUR + SUITING UP

What areas of your life has the enemy been attacking? Have you been in fervent prayer about these situations?

Think about the armor of God and write out a prayer, asking God for the protection of his armor and for guidance through your present battlefields.

Confide in a prayer partner. "Again I say to you, if two of you agree on earth about anything they ask, it will be done for them by my Father in heaven. For where two or three are gathered in my name, there am I among them" (Matthew 18:19 ESV).

---

[1] Lexico, s.v. "fervent (a.)," accessed March 19, 2020, https://www.lexico.com/en/definition/fervent.

[2] Priscilla Shirer, *Fervent: A Woman's Battle Plan to Serious, Specific, and Strategic Prayer* (Nashville: B&H Publishing Group, 2015), 4.

[3] Shirer, *Fervent: A Woman's Battle Plan to Serious, Specific, and Strategic Prayer*, 15-17.

[4] Robert Gobelet, *Questions and Answers From The Bible* (lulu.com, 2017), 358-359.

[5] Gobelet, *Questions and Answers From The Bible, 364.*

[6] Gobelet, *Questions and Answers From The Bible,*

[7] Shirer, *Fervent: A Woman's Battle Plan to Serious, Specific, and Strategic Prayer*, 5.

CHAPTER ELEVEN

# IN THE END

Paul was a man of faith. As I study his letters, I am confident that when his life ended, and he came face to face with the Father, he heard, "Well done, my good and faithful servant."[1] But Paul initially rejected God's Son. In fact, he persecuted believers and was even eager to kill them.[2] Then an encounter with Jesus convinced the Jewish Pharisee that he was completely wrong.

On the day of his conversion, Paul (also known as Saul) was traveling to Damascus to hunt for Jesus-followers. He intended to arrest them (both men and women). Suddenly, a blinding light came down from heaven, and Saul heard a voice say, "Saul! Saul! Why are you persecuting me?" Saul responds, "Who are you, lord?" And the voice replied, "I am Jesus, the one you are persecuting!"[3]

At that moment, Saul discerned that Jesus was who He claimed to be. How fearful Saul must have been, paralyzed by this realization! He had stubbornly carried the weight of a hardened heart, and now he sensed the seriousness of his sin.

> *Saul's Conversion*
>
> *The men with Saul stood speechless, for they heard the sound of someone's voice but saw no one! Saul picked himself up off the ground, but when he opened his eyes he was blind. So his companions led him by the hand to Damascus. He remained there blind for three days and did not eat or drink. Now there was a believer in Damascus named Ananias. The Lord spoke to him in a vision, calling, "Ananias!" "Yes, Lord!" he replied. The Lord said, "Go over to Straight Street, to the house of Judas. When you get there, ask for a man from Tarsus named Saul. He is praying to me right now. I have shown him a vision of a man named Ananias coming in and laying hands on him so he can see again." "But Lord," exclaimed Ananias, "I've heard many people talk about the terrible things this man has done to the believers in Jerusalem! And he is authorized by the leading priests to arrest everyone who calls upon your name. "But the Lord said, "Go, for Saul is my chosen instrument to take my message to the Gentiles and to kings, as well as to the people of Israel. (Acts 9:7-15)*

After his conversion, Saul immediately "began preaching about Jesus in the synagogues, saying, 'He is indeed the Son of God!'" (Acts 9:20). Saul continued to preach and was sent on a mission by the Holy Spirit. This would be the first of four missionary journeys.[4] Despite his sordid history, Saul was chosen to go and share God's message. We are called as believers to do the same. I daresay that after reading about Paul's beginning, we are without excuse regarding our past. Paul was hell-bent down the wrong path, but Jesus mercifully stopped him at a crossroad on his way to Damascus and gave him a second chance.

We have been chosen, and we are commanded to make disciples. We do this by sharing our stories. We become effective witnesses by sharing what God has done in our lives.

"But you are not like that, for you are a chosen people. You are royal priests, a holy nation, God's very own possession. As a result, you can show others the goodness of God, for he called you out of the darkness into his wonderful light" (1 Peter 2:9). "You have been set apart as holy to the Lord your God, and he has chosen you from all the nations of the earth to be his own special treasure" (Deuteronomy 14:2).

Throughout Paul's missionary journeys, he passionately proclaimed that Jesus is the Way, the Truth, and the Life,[5] and he shared his own story. As a result, Paul faced much opposition and went through many trials because of his faith. But he pressed on. His heart hurt for the lost who were putting their hope in false gods and false teaching. Paul continued to share the good news, even after he was stoned to the point of near-death in Iconium.[6] He was imprisoned in multiple cities, yet he used that time to write letters. In those letters, he encouraged, taught, and mentored church members. During his last journey, Paul knew his death was imminent. Below are his last words to the elders of a church at Ephesus:

*Paul Meets the Ephesian Elders*

*When they arrived he declared, "You know that from the day I set foot in the province of Asia until now I have done the Lord's work humbly and with many tears. I have endured the trials that came to me from the plots of the Jews. I never shrank back from telling you what you needed to hear, either publicly or in your homes. I have had one message for Jews and Greeks alike—the necessity of repenting from sin and turning to God, and of having faith in our Lord Jesus. And now I am bound by the Spirit to go to Jerusalem. I don't know what awaits me, except that the Holy Spirit tells me in city after city that jail and suffering lie ahead. But my life is worth nothing to me unless I use it for finishing the work assigned me by the Lord Jesus—the work of*

> *telling others the Good News about the wonderful grace of God." (Acts 20:18-24)*

Are you allowing Him to use your thorns? Are you sharing about God's grace in your life?

We know by Paul's letter in 2 Corinthians that our walk is going to be hard. We may come to crossroads in life and feel faint, looking at the obstacles in front of us. But that's when we must stand firm in our faith and focus on Jesus. He will help us finish the course like He helped Paul. "I have fought the good fight, I have finished the race, and I have remained faithful" (2 Timothy 4:7).

As we maneuver through life and all it throws at us, we are bound to be burdened by thorns in the flesh. Our thorns are painful reminders of hard times -- maybe a period of depression, the loss of a child, or experiencing infidelity. But God wants us to share our stories about how He has given us victory over those things. Our stories are ultimately meant to bring glory to God. Paul is the supreme example. He was consistent in sharing about the forgiveness of sins through Jesus. He aimed to show God's grace and love to all, and God used him (despite his sins, his thorns, and his guilt) to become one of the greatest ministers of all time. And think about how much of the New Testament was penned by Paul. God's glory is still growing from those books.

Are you testifying to the Good News about the wonderful grace of God?

Paul boldly shared his testimony with King Agrippa in the following passage:

> *Paul Speaks to Agrippa*
>
> *Then Agrippa said to Paul, "You may speak in your defense." So Paul, gesturing with his hand, started his defense: "I am fortunate, King*

*Agrippa, that you are the one hearing my defense today against all these accusations made by the Jewish leaders, for I know you are an expert on all Jewish customs and controversies. Now please listen to me patiently! As the Jewish leaders are well aware, I was given a thorough Jewish training from my earliest childhood among my own people and in Jerusalem. If they would admit it, they know that I have been a member of the Pharisees, the strictest sect of our religion. Now I am on trial because of my hope in the fulfillment of God's promise made to our ancestors. In fact, that is why the twelve tribes of Israel zealously worship God night and day, and they share the same hope I have. Yet, Your Majesty, they accuse me for having this hope! Why does it seem incredible to any of you that God can raise the dead? I used to believe that I ought to do everything I could to oppose the very name of Jesus the Nazarene. Indeed, I did just that in Jerusalem. Authorized by the leading priests, I caused many believers there to be sent to prison. And I cast my vote against them when they were condemned to death. Many times I had them punished in the synagogues to get them to curse Jesus. I was so violently opposed to them that I even chased them down in foreign cities. One day I was on such a mission to Damascus, armed with the authority and commission of the leading priests. About noon, Your Majesty, as I was on the road, a light from heaven brighter than the sun shone down on me and my companions. We all fell down, and I heard a voice saying to me in Aramaic, 'Saul, Saul, why are you persecuting me? It is useless for you to fight against my will.' 'Who are you, lord?' I asked. And the Lord replied, 'I am Jesus, the one you are persecuting. Now get to your feet! For I have appeared to you to appoint you as my servant and witness. Tell people that you have seen me, and tell them what I will show you in the future. And I will rescue you from both your own people and the Gentiles. Yes, I am sending you to the Gentiles to open their eyes, so they may turn from darkness to light and from the power of Satan to God. Then they will receive forgiveness for their sins and be given a place among God's people, who are set apart by faith in me.' And so, King Agrippa, I obeyed that vision from heaven. I preached first to those in Damascus, then in Jerusalem and throughout all Judea, and also to the Gentiles, that all must repent of their sins and turn to God—*

> *and prove they have changed by the good things they do. Some Jews arrested me in the Temple for preaching this, and they tried to kill me. But God has protected me right up to this present time so I can testify to everyone, from the least to the greatest. I teach nothing except what the prophets and Moses said would happen—that the Messiah would suffer and be the first to rise from the dead, and in this way announce God's light to Jews and Gentiles alike. (Acts 26:1-23)*

Notice that Paul described himself before knowing Christ, his conversion to Christ, and how he had been blessed by Christ since following Him. Your testimony does not have to be long or dramatic, but it can contain these elements. If you accepted Jesus at a young age, then your testimony will primarily be about your life with Christ. The most compelling part of your story will be how your life has changed since accepting Jesus as your Savior, or how Jesus gives you hope. Be thinking about that because I'm going to challenge you to write it out.

I've noticed four excuses that prevent people from talking about their faith.

1. They don't think their story is interesting.
2. They don't feel comfortable declaring their story.
3. They haven't noticed how God has been at work in their life.
4. They fear being judged.

Allow Paul to inspire you. Like him, we should enthusiastically go to homes, communities, other states, and even to other countries, proclaiming God's goodness. Despite the fact that Paul knew he would probably die a martyr, he bravely continued to attest that Jesus is the Messiah.

Remember the woman at the well? She knew her neighbors didn't like her. She knew people were suspicious of her, because of her sinful past. But she chose to share Jesus with her community anyway. She literally ran to them, a group that despised her, to tell them about Jesus!

Because of Paul and the Samaritan woman, many people came to know Jesus as their Lord and Savior. They became effective witnesses by simply speaking. Friends, we must be ready to share Truth with those who are searching for it. Contribute to God's kingdom by conversing with others. "If someone asks about your hope as a believer, always be ready to explain it" (1 Peter 3:15).

---

[1] Matthew 25:21
[2] Acts 9:1
[3] Acts 9:4-5
[4] Acts 13
[5] John 14:6
[6] Acts 14:19

CHAPTER TWELVE

# YOUR THORNS, YOUR STORY

Like Paul, we are going to walk through thorny trials, but that is a part of life. God will use difficult experiences to sanctify us—to make us more like Christ. Remember that our strength comes from Him. Don't forget that your story is beautiful and uniquely yours! God gave it to you, and no one else.

Where are you now? Are you following Christ? Have you accepted Him as your Lord and Savior? If yes, that's wonderful! I wish I had the opportunity to sit with you and hear your story and how God is using you. If you haven't yet accepted Christ into your heart, what is stopping you?

Can you relate to my fear of not being accepted into a church community because of my past? I worried about that before accepting Christ. I wrestled with the skeletons in my closet and the sin in my life, but I couldn't shake the conviction which consumed me. God planted that conviction, and He pursued me until I accepted Him. Now that I believe in the work of Christ on the cross and His resurrection, a weight has been lifted. I now stand confident, knowing my sins have been forgiven because Jesus paid the penalty. Instead of feeling separated from the Father, I am now His adopted daughter. And I know He will never leave me.

This confidence and security gave me the courage to step into ministry, despite skepticism. I stood before my doubters, knowing that my heart was transformed. Remember, this is your story and your relationship with Christ, no one else's. I am reminded of an incident that John recorded, which happened at the temple in Jerusalem. Some teachers of religious law and Pharisees brought in a woman who was caught in the act of adultery. They put her in front of the crowd there, and asked Jesus, "'This woman was caught in the act of adultery. The law of Moses says to stone her. What do you say?' They were trying to trap him into saying something they could use against him, but Jesus stooped down and wrote in the dust with his finger. They kept demanding an answer, so he stood up again and said, 'All right, but let the one who has never sinned throw the first stone!'" (John 8:4-7).

In this passage, Jesus clearly asserts that no one is without sin, and no sin is greater than any other sin. The crowd quietly agreed, each slipping away from the scene in silence. "Then Jesus stood up again and said to the woman, 'Where are your accusers? Didn't even one of them condemn you?' 'No, Lord,' she said. And Jesus said, 'Neither do I. Go and sin no more'" (John 8:10-11). Don't you love that? These are His words to us, also!

## REFLECTION FIVE + YOUR STORY

What is holding you back from following Christ? Could it be something related to a crossroad that you wrote down in Chapter Seven? If it's something you're ashamed of, ask God in the name of Jesus to forgive you. Allow Him to take your baggage, so you can freely run forward for His glory!



It's a lot to think about—life, that is. I imagine many things are running through your head. What are you hearing from the Holy Spirit, and what might the enemy be whispering to you? Satan does not want you to be a messenger of Christ. The evil one will do anything he can to keep you from sharing God's grace and love. Try to decipher where your thoughts are coming from. Is the enemy planting insecurities and excuses in your mind? What is God the Holy Spirit saying to you?

Enemy -



God -

Like Paul, I became a believer later in life. What about you? If you've already accepted Jesus as your Savior, describe in several sentences how that came to be. How old were you? Where were you, and who helped lead you to the Lord?

God seized Paul's attention by blinding him and then healing him. This miracle proved to Paul that Jesus defeated death and is alive. As a result, Paul could no longer deny the divine identity of Christ. Was there a pivotal point in your life that made you recognize the reality of God? Were you at a crossroad pondering which path to take?

After receiving Christ, we can still encounter dark tunnels of doubt or scary circumstances along life's journey. Are you at such a place now? Is it causing you to question your faith?

If so, what happened (or is happening)?

Are you calling on God for guidance and answers, or are you questioning His goodness and love for you?

If you are at a difficult roadblock, I encourage you to find a believer to confide in. We are called to be part of a unified body of believers. This means being a church member and walking through life with brothers and sisters in Christ. Talk to a friend or church elder and seek refuge in God's Word. Paul encouraged believers to "Share each other's burdens, and in this way obey the law of Christ" (Galatians 6:2).

Since becoming a follower of Christ, how have you seen Him move in your life?

How have you changed (your heart, how you talk, how you see the world, etc.)?

What is He doing in your life right now?

Sharing our stories with the world is how we spread the Gospel, and it's how we fulfill the Great Commission. Jesus said, "Go into all the world and preach the Good News to everyone" (Mark 16:15). Be honest about where you are in your faith walk, but give credit and glory to God for the good in your life and the hope you have. Just doing that can be eye-opening and encouraging to others. Think about how convincing it is to hear the same thing from two different people. Try to be the first or second person who gives praise to Jesus in front of someone. Doing that would show how powerful He is. It would display His grace to someone who is rejecting Jesus. Tell someone they are chosen and loved by their Creator when they are feeling alone.

I praise Him every day for what He has done in my life. I have made peace with my past, knowing it is what propelled me to Jesus and the life I now live. In the space below, I encourage you to write out your testimony, compiling your answers to the previous questions. Aim for a four- to five-minute story that glorifies God. Challenge yourself to share it. Ask a believing friend to share her story with you. Practice with one another. Don't skip this exercise; it's an essential part of following Christ.

My Story -

God wants you to share your testimony. My thorns still poke and irritate me, but God's power within me will enable me to do great things in spite of my weaknesses. I believe that, and you should believe the same for yourself. Please don't close this book without that perspective. Do not let the enemy use your thorns to keep you complacent. Instead, allow God to work through you from now on for His glory!

Thank you for reading my story. I am sincerely grateful, and in return, I've written a prayer for you.

*Father God, I come to You, lifting up each person who is reading this prayer. Father, you know who they are, and you know their story. You have observed them at crossroads, and you know about the thorns they tolerate. I pray that You will empower them to tell their story with the intentions of bringing glory to You and advancing Your kingdom. As we come to crossroads in life, keep our eyes fixed on You. Father, I pray for the people who feel stuck. Bless them with at least one believer who will encourage them in their walk with You. Equip them with verses from Your Word. When life is overwhelming, help us see You at work. Strengthen us. When marriage is hard, when children are sick, when addictions consume, when depression or anxiety strike, and when You feel distant, help us to see You. Remove the blinders! Help us see your grace between our thorns and the beauty in that. Father, give my friends the courage to step forward in faith and finish the course you've laid out for them. May we give You praise every chance we get. We love You! Thank You for sending Your Son to die on the cross for our sins. Continue to transform our hearts and open our eyes. We want to be more like Jesus. In His name, I pray. Amen!*

# ABOUT THE AUTHOR

Cheryl Goss is a women's conference speaker, Bible teacher, encourager, and founder of Connecting Ministries (connectingministries.org). She is passionate about helping women find their own passions and gifts by claiming the story God has given them. Cheryl's mission, personally and through Connecting Ministries, is to reach all women, regardless of denomination, generation, or background. She wants to connect with each woman she meets on a personal level and make them feel comfortable, accepted, and loved. Cheryl strives to share God's Word in a way that meets women where they are, so they leave encouraged and wanting more of Him. She and her husband Ryan have four children: Timothy, Peyton, Layla, and Mia.

Made in the USA
Columbia, SC
08 October 2020